CHANGING
MIND

VINCENT G. STUART

CHANGING
MIND

1981
SHAMBHALA
BOSTON & LONDON

Shambhala Publications, Inc.
300 Massachusetts Avenue
Boston, Massachusetts 02115

© 1981 by Vincent G. Stuart
Distributed in the United States by Random House
and in Canada by Random House of Canada Ltd.

Distributed in the United Kingdom by Routledge &
Kegan Paul Ltd., London and Henley-on-Thames

Printed in the United States of America

LIBRARY OF CONGRESS CATALOGING IN PUBLICATION DATA

Stuart, Vincent G.
  Changing mind.
    1. Spiritual life. 2. Occult sciences. I. Title.
BL624.S78   291.4'2   80-53447
ISBN 0-87773-206-X
ISBN 0-394-51791-1 (Random House)
BVG 01

CONTENTS

Introduction

THIS book is written for those who are on the verge of looking for an esoteric teaching, or who are about to join a school. Its intention is to prepare the minds of such people for the reception of ideas that can transform their beings. It points out that certain qualities are necessary to form the ground in which esoteric ideas may be sown, and that a candidate for a school should first have made every effort, to the best of his ability, to have developed his faculties.

It must be realised that the acquirement of new knowledge is not in itself sufficient to effect transformation of being, nor do schools, if genuine, attempt to transform pupils. Transformation begins with transformation of the understanding, something that occurs when ideas are applied to being and their truth is perceived for oneself. Transformation is a process of self-development, willingly and spontaneously practised. Esoteric teachings contain the knowledge of how to transform one's being. They point the way, but their application is voluntary, for transformation of being is a voluntary task of self-development.

I wish to acknowledge my teacher, the late Dr Maurice Nicoll, from whose writings I quote, and to whom I owe my understanding of the idea of transformation in general and of the Work in particular.

Extracts from the work of Dr Maurice Nicoll are reprinted with the permission of Watkins Publishing, Bridge Street, Dulverton, Somerset, England, for Mrs Isobel Salole.

1

I. Wonder

ESOTERIC teaching is for those who have the conviction that life cannot be understood in terms of itself, but that there must be some kind of knowledge that leads to an understanding of life.

It is indispensable to have a sense of wonder, which lies in the places of the emotions where worth and valuation are felt, that can distinguish the difference between the influences and knowledge of man's physical life and occupations, and the influences and knowledge that speak of man's possible destiny. If we feel that reality is only in the world of the senses, in the ever-turning kaleidoscope of confusion, then we shall not be moved by the spirit of esotericism. The conviction that the meaning of life exists and the sense of wonder that in the universe and in ourselves there is the *raison d' être* of 'creation' are attributes of being, possessed by some people and not by others—not in those described by Christ as having ears that do not hear and eyes that do not see. Without these attributes, intellect alone would seek to add to our sum of knowledge, and thus to a continuing state of confusion, because esoteric knowledge would be judged as just another branch of sense-based knowledge. It is only the sense of wonder that enables intellect to realise that esotericism is an altogether different kind of knowledge from that which is sense-based and commonly called logical, whereas esotericism is about our psychology. Everyone has a psychology, but it is not easily admitted, for one's own or another person's psychology cannot be seen or touched

3

by the outer senses. Yet we have the power to think psychologically once we have seen that the human mind by its sense-based thinking contributes to its own enslavement. Logical and literal thinking puts psychological understanding to death. Psychologically we are our understanding, and through the application of an esoteric teaching to our psychological being, our understanding of ourselves and of life in general increases. Thus begins the evolution of our psychology.

When we wonder what our life and interests mean from a feeling that something is missing, that there is a certain meaninglessness, even, in everything experienced hitherto, however responsibly we have met our obligations, we may feel very empty. If, at the same time, we feel that our own individuality, something that is truly ourselves, has never grown but has remained latent, unborn, within us, we may begin to see that we have been overpowered by outer life and influenced mainly by all that acts upon us from the outside. The part of us from which we can grow has been lost. If we desire to find the meaning of our lives we may then realise, if we think deeply enough, that it is necessary to find and follow a spiritual discipline, a system proceeding according to definite laws that will bring order into our being, transforming us from a machine driven by the senses into another kind of person, the realisation of whose essential individuality is the aim of our existence.

We may have come to recognise the bewildering changes in our moods, from degrees of happiness to degrees of depression, but we have little, if any, idea that these are the signature of our being. We cannot see being and do not know how to see

4

what or who controls it. We realise that we need some special kind of guidance to enable us to understand who and what we are; that is, that as well as being composed of flesh and blood and bones we are composed of invisible thoughts, feelings, and impulses that determine the quality of our disordered psychology. 'But while the given physical body is ordered and can work harmoniously the psychological body is not given and is by no means ordered. From this point of view Man's task is to bring about order in the psychological body which is in disorder' (Maurice Nicoll, *The Mark*, London, 1954).

In order to understand what is meant by psychology, it is first necessary to know that 'esoteric psychology and its great distinction from Western psychology lies in the fact that it does not regard man as being conscious. Esoteric psychology regards man as being in a state of sleep in which everything happens to him, a state in which he imagines that he is conscious, a state in which he imagines he has Will, in which he imagines he has a permanent ego and in which he imagines he can do. Esoteric psychology teaches us that all this is illusion and that Man attributes to himself what he does not possess' (Maurice Nicoll, *Psychological Commentaries on the Teaching of G.I. Gurdjieff & P.D. Ouspensky*, London, 1952). This is a truth not evident to the sense-based mind and will be strongly denied by those for whom literal and logical proof is the only kind of truth. People who are moved by the spirit of esotericism will already have an inkling of the difference between esoteric and Western psychology.

Finding an authentic teaching and a teacher is a task for the discriminative, cognitive power of the inner emotions. Being without psychological awareness of teachings and teachers, the intellect has no means of exercising its comparative faculty and making a choice. But it may well attempt to do so, and, lacking the insight into people and ideas possessed by the same parts of the emotions which can feel worth and valuation, make a naïve mistake. It is therefore necessary to trust the discriminative, cognitive power of the inner emotions, acting as a radar, to find the authentic teaching and the teacher. If, however, the cognition of the emotions is superimposed by imagination, it cannot exercise its proper function. As a result, imagination will project its idea of a teaching and a teacher upon some corresponding individual and his system. It has to be admitted that it is one's own psychological being that makes a right or wrong choice, and hence it is one's own responsibility. One may be influenced by the opinions of other people, by the books one has read, for example; but the final choice must be decided by one's own inner discrimination, for it is one's own being that decides the question. The choice proves whether or not one is ready for a genuine teacher and teaching. There is no infallible outer safeguard against making a wrong choice, but a modicum of common sense is helpful.

*   *   *

Although the transformation of our psychology cannot proceed from the sphere of sense knowledge, it is nevertheless the ordinary intellect that has to record, at first, the ideas presented by an esoteric teaching. Nor can the transformation proceed before the physical body, the emotions, the intellect, and the instincts have received sufficient training in the first education to develop their material capabilities. Although flesh, blood, and bones are given as a vehicle for the psychological being, we will eventually come to realise that there is no 'he' or 'she' who thinks, feels, desires, and so on. However, there is an acquired personality that supposedly thinks, feels, and desires, that is governed by reactions to outer events and inner thoughts and feelings formed by upbringing and schooling, by theories, dogmas, and prejudices of history, by nationality, religion, and social caste, by every mass emotion and mental attitudes fashionable of the day. None of these reactions, all answering to the name of 'I', are our selves. If knowledge of the ideas of transformation results in a mechanical rejection of everything connected with our upbringing and first necessary schooling, which have formed the apparatus of the mechanical psychology, only the imaginary idea of ourselves is increased. Nothing in a teaching becomes animated until its truth has been proved for ourselves, by applying it as directed.

Paradoxically, although the sense-based mind cannot understand the psychological, the spiritual level above itself, it must first be trained in the principle of effort, as must all the attributes of the physical man, in order to understand that everything from smallest to largest is organised, that is to say, is on a scale of levels with the requisite energy to function. In learning the principle of effort we learn that much more energy can be received by the physical and psychological man when he makes every effort to attune his faculties to a high degree of activity. The higher forces latent in our psychological being are realised only when our faculties are sufficiently developed. What has not been trained cannot be activated; the organism is stunted and impoverished. Were we, in this condition, to attempt to impose sensual thinking on psychological truth, everything in us that could lead to internal development would be destroyed, because the sensual mind is incapable of understanding this kind of truth and would misinterpret it to such a degree that it would become false. Thus, the emotions would receive the wrong message, resulting in the fortifying, instead of the diminishment, of the imaginary self.

When it is fully understood that, in order to learn the principle of effort, a reasonable attainment of the capacities for living in the physical world must precede any attempt to bring order into the psychological world, it is easier to apply new ideas to our being. In the external, physical world effort is involuntary, but in the psychological world transformation of being is voluntary; that is to say, it is not necessary for leading a mechanical existence. In following a teaching we therefore practise voluntarily a discipline extra to the discipline exacted by external and physical circumstances. Only insofar as this extra discipline is willingly practised does it animate the individual's awareness.

The principle of effort can be learned by making a thorough study of a particular subject. It will then be perceived that there are laws regulating the development of its entity through stages, or levels, of greater and greater complexity, or of finer and finer refinement, and that if the laws are disrupted or not observed, its inherent possibilities cannot be harmoniously completed. In other words, in studying the nature and laws of aim, cause, and effect common to all subjects, it may be recognised that the same *principle* of laws governs the transformation of being when it is deliberately and voluntarily practised. In the case of human beings, that is to say, ourselves, it is our entity, or essence, that becomes the subject capable of achieving harmonious development by means of precise efforts defined by the teaching being administered unto us and voluntarily practised by ourselves.

Through applying ourselves to the study and practise of a particular subject, we begin to see that nothing is attainable without effort and that the principle of effort is universal. Once this has become clear, it is less difficult to recognise that without deliberate effort the many sides of ourselves cannot be harmonised. In making this effort it is very likely that we begin to become aware, for the first time, of the very existence of our psychology and of some of the factors of which it is constituted. We shall find that although one part of ourselves wishes to make effort and is interested, there are many other parts that are unwilling, bored, and indifferent. From this experience we may gain an inkling that apparently we have something other and more than a sense-based mind; that we have more than one will; that we are something that hitherto has been clothed with the thoughts, desires, and feelings that we have assumed are our own. Possibly it may now occur to us that transformation has something to do with becoming aware of all the activities—reactions—that go on in our being without our control or knowledge, even, and with voiding ourselves of the illusion that they are 'I, myself'. Instead of seeing people, ideas, things, *etcetera*, through associations and attitudes implanted in us since childhood, we may be able to obtain a direct impression of them. In short, if we reflect deeply enough, we may realise that if we are to come into a new state of ourselves we need to discover how to disengage from the power of old habits—mental, emotional, and physical.

Frequently this insight into ourselves comes in a momentary, vivid flash. All at once we know a state of animation that is incomparably quicker than even our most exalted moods, and remember it as if it were something that had been lost and forgotten: there is a conviction that given the chance to breathe, there is a real self waiting to be acknowledged. Should the 'taste' of this experience endure, it will reinforce the will of the inner emotions to regain permanently the integration with the real self momentarily shown to us. It may also come as a shock to us to realize that when this real self is not present, our life lacks conscious direction and is subject to haphazard accident. But the will of the inner emotions is far from being the only will in our being: there are many wills, each with its own values, interests and motives, concerned with their own presumed advantages. Hence, however intense has been the experience of self-recollection with its power to energize the emotional will, it cannot be taken for granted that the other wills wish to participate in the effort to be wholly and permanently our real self, as we shall discover later on, or that they can understand what is implied by the sudden presence of energies never before experienced. Whether or not we have attained a quality of being that will constitute a ground fertile enough to germinate a seed of esoteric truth will be shown by our subsequent attitude. The parable of the sower and the seed clearly describes in imagery how in some people the truth and good of a teaching prospers and how in others there is no harvest.

If we grasp that without some special kind of knowledge we are incapable of realising this real self that has been shown to us in a flash, and above all, if it has now become of supreme importance to us to find this self that has been lost, it is then that the teaching that will minister to our particular psychology is likely to be met. Again, this depends upon our readiness to accept the answer that the universe sends in reply to the questions we have formulated in respect to the meaning of our own lives and of human life in general. If these fundamental questions are of merely passing curiosity—mental toys—a brush with a teaching, should one be met, leaves the imaginary self, the ego, more entrenched than before. Fortunately, as man can indeed undergo a transformation of being through conscious suffering and voluntary effort, there are teachings for those who are ready to receive them, guiding us how to realise the essential birthright by first of all becoming conscious that our mechanical personality and its psychology are not conscious.

The first source of meaning has been gained through the perception of the senses, and it is the reactions of the senses that pass for consciousness and qualify our understanding. If we can accept the teaching of esoteric psychology that we are not conscious but can become so, the principles and meaning of esoteric ideas contain the spermatic force that will emancipate us from the sensual mentality, that is to say, from our hard and fast prejudices, associations, attitudes, and habits. Our relatively few ways of experiencing life will thus be increased. Consequently, our being will be enriched by the ability to receive energy from a greater compass of impressions. When we have learned how to take these impressions consciously, their energy becomes transformed into a psychological force that can contribute towards a state of self-recollection. In making it possible for someone to think beyond the evidence of the senses, the object is not to destroy the meanings on that level, but to open other levels of meaning not perceptible to the senses. This requires us to realise that there are different levels of meaning, that there is a scale of meaning; for without the perception of scales and levels things are made to appear opposite, and so lead to endless arguments and confusion. Sense-based thinking is on one level; psychological thinking is on another; they are not opposites.

No one who takes everything literally can think psychologically. The literal mind cannot understand that the language used in Christ's parables, for example, is symbolical and allegorical, describing the inward psychological characteristics of a person—his or her present state. Unless we realise that we take ourselves for granted, that we can speak, think, move, see, or hear without having any idea how to explain all this, we shall lack that sense of wonder that could cause us to begin to reflect on our lives and the kind of people we have been, in such a way that there begins to be a separation of the internal from the external. Without meditating on the inexplicability of everything, including ourselves, we shall not reach a state of understanding—quite different from our ordinary everyday understanding—that can inspire us to begin the evolution of what is truly our self.

The intellect of a person who can think psychologically should be able to assess truth and discriminate between truth and falsity; the emotions should be able to descry whether or not there is good in the truth of esoteric ideas, for without feeling the good the truth is not willed. In our present violent world, where good is seldom valued and truth is twisted into lies, the will seeks what it regards as its own good, according to its own nature, so that all wars, all conflicts, all actions called bad and evil are someone's idea of good. But there is a good that does not reside in the self-emotions—the only kind of emotion we usually feel—but which is the quality of a level within us called in Christianity 'The Kingdom of Heaven' and in Buddhism 'Enlightenment'. Although we can sometimes feel the presence of this good, our consciousness is not yet at a level where our whole being is equal to it, sometimes described as 'The Perfected Man', a level on which all that is psychologi-

13

cally material has been overcome. Christianity admonishes us to seek first the Kingdom of Heaven and tells us emphatically that it is within us, *now*. To realise this quality of being, intellect and emotions must first be developed and united.

II. Levels of Being

'MAN is created a self-developing organism, as a seed that can grow upwards in the vertical scale of being, and from the higher level that creates man comes all esoteric teaching—that is, the eternal teaching about Man and his possible inner evolution and the means whereby this can be attained' (Maurice Nicoll, *The Mark*, London, 1954).

The gist of this idea exists in all esoteric teachings. Its transformative power is effective only for those people who can respond to its good and who, having struggled to find the meaning of themselves and of the universe, realise that a certain kind of help is required, but not the kind of 'help' desired by the level which expects to be nursed, to be mothered, to be 'saved' by someone else, be it Christ or Buddha. That kind of 'help' only puts us even more to sleep. The help we need is the knowledge of how to awaken ourselves and the surveillance that this knowledge is being applied correctly.

'It is impossible to understand esoteric ideas on the most literal, mechanical level of the mind. Yet, at the same time, they must to some extent fall first on this level, for no one can think in a new way unless he starts from what he knows and understands already' (*ibid.*). This being evident to a teacher, his concern is whether or not the person presenting himself as a pupil has the potential capacity to receive esoteric ideas and germinate them. He himself is a responsible trustee of esoteric ideas and therefore must assure himself that the people to whom he passes on the knowledge of inner evolution will not suc-

15

cumb to the temptation to use the knowledge to gain power for themselves. A teacher who does not heed this responsibility shows himself to be a charlatan desirous of mass adulation.

Whenever mankind is in an extra-critical condition—at the end of an age, at the nadir of a cycle of civilisation—esoteric ideas are widely sown, one reason being that their influence keeps alive the notion that there is a higher level of civilisation than the level to which mankind has degenerated. Another reason is that mankind, as part of organic life, is required to serve as a transmitter of energy to levels of being lower down the scale of creation, and unless reminded that there is a higher level of being that can be reached by conscious effort, mankind would be drawn down into subhuman reproduction. The influence that esoteric ideas exert upon the life of humanity radiates through people whose real conscience has become their spiritual director. Although, by the majority of people, this influence is received as unconsciously as is the influence of the planets, it nevertheless counters, to some extent, the influences governing the descent of mankind's being. The exoteric doctrine of the various churches exhorts mankind to observe a standard of conduct that people used to recognise as ideal, even if they paid it only lip-service. At least it was an influence for a certain kind of good beyond self-interest, and was represented as conscience. Taking the representation as being real conscience, every individual in every generation has adapted the doctrine after his own comprehension and convenience, so that there are as many concepts of conscience, hardly distinguishable from self-love, as there are individuals. Instead of uniting humanity, these so-called consciences are the bases of every kind of dispute—between individuals, between classes, between generations, between political parties, between religions, and between nations.

Mankind's history is a recurrent cycle of the rising and falling of civilisation after civilisation. Now one nation and now another rises and falls: the pattern of ascent-descent-ascent-descent continually repeats itself at the level of the universe called Earth. No human being can change the laws ordering the universe, but an individual can learn how to transform himself, and he, being a point in the universe, makes it possible for another to move up the scale of being if he succeeds in transforming himself. For those people who come to realise that this self-transformation requires a special kind of knowledge are probably ready to meet an esoteric teaching.

III. Scale and the Different Minds

A T whatever age we may be when we feel that some essential meaning is missing from our lives and interests, before the process of evolution can start it is not only necessary to believe in something higher than ourselves, but to be able to meet the ordinary responsibilities of daily life adequately. This 'something higher than ourselves' is not an external force or authority, or person, but a potential, latent level of our own being, its degree of full realisation known, for example, as Christ or Buddha. If it is claimed that belief in something higher than ourselves excuses the observance of ordinary responsibilities, then in fact nothing but extreme self-conceit and egoism is our highest concern. For Western man, esoteric studies and the affairs of daily life have both to be undertaken, as, eventually, a new way of living in life is to be practised.

One of the properties of psychological thinking gives the appreciation of the existence and meaning of scale: for example, it enables us to perceive that the universe consists of levels of quality, levels of intelligence, levels of uses, and to apprehend that in ourselves there is a parallel scale. This perception opens the mind to the realisation that evolution is on the vertical scale and does not lie along the horizontal line of 'progress'. Our being contains all possible levels of being; in each of us there is a common factor, a feature that characterises the levels as a whole and gives us a recognisable distinction, albeit with a mechanical psychology. The laws governing the different levels of the universe, including this earth and the life upon it, may be likened to the laws of the musical octave, and we, as part of organic life, are subject to the same laws. Just as these laws maintain a given universe, so do they maintain our physical body, with which, for the most part, we are identified. Consequently, our so-called consciousness is an automatic reaction to the constantly changing conditions of identification with the personality's functions. In short, it is the fragmented response of the natural man to the laws governing organic life. As this happens without our awareness or control or choice, esotericism calls it a state of sleep.

Carried within the physical body, as an oak tree within an acorn, there is the seed of our essential being and its potentialities, as described in the parable of the sower and the seed. This is the part of us that can realise its inherent 'perfected' condition if we awaken from our imaginary consciousness. This awakening is the possible inner evolution of self-development. Although not directly under the laws governing the physical body and psychology, the seed of essential being cannot germinate as long as the idea and meaning of ourselves are based on the imaginary consciousness. The personality, consequent upon this imaginary consciousness, usurps the right of essence, keeping it inactive. As true consciousness is the means by which essence can become active, we have to find laws and influences that can gradually help to diminish the illusionary idea and meaning of ourselves, so as to liberate essence from the domination of the personality. The laws and influences of true consciousness are expounded in esoteric teachings, evoking real conscience from whence comes the strength to persist in the process by which the real self evolves.

* * *

We do not realise that we have more than one mind, that that mind is not simply some kind of adjunct to the brain. What, for example, controls the working and ordering of the physical body, its movements and instincts? What controls the emotions? Is there a mind for each, or are they mindless?

We have the mind of the intellect, the mind of the emotions, the mind of the instincts conjoined with the mind of bodily movement, and the mind of sex. Of these different minds only the mind of instinct is active at birth. But are we aware of these several minds and their potentialities? Do we know how they can be developed? They have been given to us to enable us to adapt to life, but we rarely develop their capacities and thus remain but rough sketches of a human being. Before we are ready to be accepted by an esoteric school there is much preparatory work for us to do: for instance, to learn the uses of the different minds and begin to equip them for development. From applying ourselves to this study, we can begin to realise that the principle of scale and order, through voluntary effort, can be introduced into our psychology, thus preparing us to receive the influences and ideas that can awaken it to real consciousness.

Transformation of our being from a state of imaginary consciousness to real consciousness requires, among other things, the development, refinement, and ordering of the faculties with which we have been endowed at birth: the minds of the intellect, the emotions, the instincts, bodily movement, and sex. All that constitutes the personality is enregistered on the faculties as music is enregistered on a record, such as opinions, facts, and knowledge, qualified by gender, nationality, religion, social strata, parental and school upbringing, the general climate of ideas, the theories, fads, and fashions of our generation, books, plays, films, politics, money, business, wars, *etcetera*. The first education does not train our faculties equally, and generally there is a tendency for one particular faculty, whether or not it be appropriate, to cope with all kinds of situations. The reason for this becomes apparent as gradually we begin to know ourselves.

Whatever may be the actual reason for one human being to differ in character from another—whether it be due to karma, or to essence choosing its lot, as Plato describes the rewards of justice after death in the myth of Er—it is not too difficult to see that *some* differences can be accounted for in the degree of training and the sequence of reaction of the five minds. For example, there are people who are impetuous, people who think before they speak, people who feel everything very strongly, people who are governed by habitual bodily movements, people who have instinctive reactions. What is important to recognise is that the manner of relating ourselves to no-matter-what event is invariably through the predominating faculty; hence it is only by accident when it happens to be suitable. It is therefore through the very lack of consciousness that our whole life is controlled by the automatic reactions of the personality.

Until we have begun to be taught how to develop real consciousness, we rest under the illusion that we are in control of our lives and that all our choices and decisions are made consciously. Instead of remaining at the mercy of the haphazard reactions of the unequally trained and unharmonised faculties of the five minds, we need to recognise this condition and seek to balance them so that they cooperate and do not supplant one another's rôle.

These minds have, potentially, a plurality of gifts and attributes. Instinctive mind, for example, 'attends to the inner working of the organism in all its million and one details, digesting food, healing wounds, looking after the temperature, regulating the respiration and the heart-beat, making and causing the internal secretion of the glands to work in harmony, supplying this, taking away that. All this regulation is far beyond the mind of the Intellectual Centre. To be able to think of everything all together is not characteristic of the Intellectual Centre; the mind of the Intellectual Centre thinks of one thing at a time and at the most of two things, but it is almost impossible for it to think of three things.

'Then again the mind of the Intellectual Centre is quite different from the mind of the Emotional Centre. People say that the emotions are not logical. However, the emotions have their own logic and it would be a mistake to think that the logic of the Intellectual Centre is the only possible logic. To feel a situation is quite different from thinking about it. The Emotional Centre can feel, for example, the inner state of other people, which is hidden from the mind of the Intellectual Centre. The emotions can give you the knowledge of others. . . .

'Then again the Moving Centre has a different mind from any of the others. It is constantly making adjustments of the most complicated kind which are quite impossible for the Intellectual Mind to make. This is intelligent calculation. One can feel such calculation going on as it were in one's muscles. Intellectual calculation is of quite a different kind and uses the elements of intellectual thought, such as words and numbers. The intelligence of the Moving Centre, however, uses no words or numbers but yet can calculate with the most exquisite precision some complicated series of movements that will give a definite result.

'Now let us consider the centres in connection with the way they receive things. You know you can look at a beautiful picure or scene in quite different ways. You can look at a mountain as a beautiful object, in which case you have an emotional relationship to it. Or you can look at it from the standpoint of a geologist noticing what kind of rocks, etc., it is composed of, in which case you have an intellectual relationship to it. Or you can look at from the standpoint of a climber planning the line of your ascent and the amount of effort necessary, in which case you will have mainly a Moving Centre relationship to it. . . . Let us say that you know all about the technical side of films, then you will tend to look at a film from this angle and not from the emotional value of the story, and so on. The point is that everyone sees things differently and that each person can see the same things differently at different moments so that its meaning changes. A person's intelligence, in short, is made up of many different intelligences that connect with quite different meanings of the same thing' (Maurice Nicoll, *Psychological Commentaries on the Teaching of G. I. Gurdjieff and P. D. Ouspensky*, London, 1952).

It is through attention that each mind connects with a person, object, event, idea; but ordinary attention swings here and there: relative to attracted or directed attention, it is not attention at all. Therefore we notice and experience next to nothing in comparison with the perception of directed attention.

IV. Meaning

ALTHOUGH adaptability is a sign of intelligence, we are not taught in our first education that there is more than one kind of intelligence. Do we sufficiently value the elementary principle in acquiring intelligence—listening and looking? If we apply this principle our powers of attention can become acute. Not only will common sense and our fund of information increase, but also our discernment of qualities and our discrimination of levels will become refined. Having trained our attention to observe everything external to ourselves we may later appreciate that the same principle is relevant to the acquisition of knowledge of ourselves.

If genuine interest in a subject relates us to its study, we shall perceive that it has a specific place in the hierarchy of levels, sustained by laws governing the energy that animates it. Should we come to study an exposition of the laws governing the transformation of being, we shall be more readily able to recognise a parallel principle ordering our consciousness, thoughts, and emotions, whether we utilise the faculty of self-observation or meditation with the object of exonerating the real self from the imaginary and fictitious.

In certain moods it may seem simple to decide to apply ourselves to what has attracted our attention or curiosity, or aroused our sense of wonder. Were we one and the same person at all times we could keep an aim without difficulty, but as our five minds are uncoordinated, we are creatures of many moods and interests, all of which have their opposites. Moreover, there are many assumptions about ourselves whose righteousness we do not question. For example, we all have an idea that we can recognise qualities, whether it be in clothes, works of art, motorcars, food, or anything else, because we are sure that our standards are absolute for the whole of our lives, and should be those of everyone else. This makes it exceedingly difficult to recognise and admit that there are standards higher than ours. Consequently the bounds of our outlook are limited to fixed prejudices preventing the development of personality, in the first education. A personality that is too small in its range of relationships to outer life is not going to be able to give attention to ideas concerning the inner evolution of being. When necessary, therefore, expansion of the personality has to be undertaken in preparation of a level of being capable of relating to life in such a way that when we receive esoteric teaching personality can serve its directions. We must know the highest standards of excellence in external life before we are ready to be trained in the far higher excellencies of internal being.

These stages in the expansion of personality are the first attempts in making voluntary effort. Hitherto all our efforts have been dictated by the reactions of the minds in the personality, but which we have assumed to be voluntary and conscious, and this kind of effort usually leaves us feeling tired. In contrast, conscious, voluntary effort releases the psychological energy which transforms our being.

Just as looking and listening, noticing our surroundings, are the basis of intelligence, so will they also help to sensitise and develop the emotions, the basis of maturity. The emotions range from trivial, petty likes and dislikes and their mechanical expression, personal emotions, to religious and aesthetic emotions, and also have the capacity for artistic creation, to say nothing of their possible insight into people and to receive what is called 'inspiration'. Which of these is our prevailing emotion? Are we not mostly filled with some kind of personal emotion, to the neglect of the properties of the finer emotions? But how easily we become negative when these personal emotions are not satisfied, or when we are infected by other peoples' negative moods. Unfortunately we have a strong liking for negative emotions, even exalting them to a virtue, being quite unaware of their terrible psychological poison.

We ascribe to ourselves the ability to feel love for someone else, but is not this love more often than not a reflection of self-love? That is to say, we 'love' someone who flatters and increases our self-esteem, for in our condition of psychological sleep self-love is the strongest emotion we feel. Hence the hatred felt for someone who offends us. Real love, an emotion that does not turn into its opposite, requires full consciousness, in the esoteric meaning of consciousness. Yet, now and then, we do experience a flash of real emotion, a sudden vision of the actual nature of something or someone, that is given to us in complete understanding. Or again, it may be that the essential conscience, not the acquired conscience, asserts itself, as when, for example, we abstain from taking advantage of something we know to be to another person's detriment.

Among the functions of the emotions is the ability to discern qualities and appreciate values that belong both to the tangible visible world and to the invisible. These qualities affect our being and consequently influence our manner of living, possibly rendering us less materialistic and violent than those who are accomplished intellectually and instinctively. Frequently the weakness of our emotional mind permits what it knows to be true and good to be overridden and derided by our intellect. What is true to the intuition often seems false to the intellect, for we are unaware that they are not on the same level of apprehension.

Often the emotions are a centre of conflict between what is called 'Love of God' and love of self. It has been said that only 'Love of God' can overcome love of self. The term 'Love of God' signifies the recognition of a level of being far transcending the individual ego, a level where the whole being is at one. This conflict continues as long as, once again, we fail to see that these two loves are not opposites. While they are taken to be on the same level, now one, now the other will occupy our feelings; now guiltiness, now exaltation, both of which are states of hallucination, will charge our emotions.

Greek mythology, in describing the lot of heroes who succeed in their tasks and those who fail, has a living relevance to our emotional condition by showing us the nature of the internal psychological forces that determine our conduct as long as we remain in unconscious reaction to them. Yet Greek mythology is regarded, as are fairy tales, as mere fables, except to those whose sense of wonder is affected by them. These latter people may probably see that the strength of the emotions plays a crucial part in undertaking the labours of winning the golden fleece, that is to say, of finding their lost selves through the development of real consciousness. People such as these will realise that their labours entail meeting life's obligations from a totally different standpoint from that which assumes that life is an end in itself.

This new standpoint is contained in esoteric ideas that combine the wisdom of the East with the knowledge of the West, ideas that can bring about inner evolution in the midst of our outer circumstances. If we have had the good fortune to delight in fairy tales and mythology when children, our memories will be revived by an esoteric teaching. We shall recognise that each, in its own way, is talking about the same adventure, but what appeared to us, as children, as being an adventure in the external world, may now be realised as having to take place within our own essential beings.

The events in mythology and fairy tales—the misfortunes, the good fortune, the plagues and monsters that ravage a country, the kingdoms to be won, the princesses to be wooed, to be married, to be betrayed, the gods who lend their aid or who chastise the hero—all represent the characteristics and the forces animating them within us throughout the whole scale of being. Once we begin the attempt to awaken from the sleep of the senses, everything composing the natural, unconscious man or woman, and the forces governing them, have to be met and if possible, transcended by non-identifying with them.

At each level of evolution, the tasks confronting us offer opportunities to develop towards our real selves, if we are sufficiently alert to recognise, as, for instance, *The Tibetan Book*

of the Dead tells us, that these tasks occur because our unconscious personality projects them into manifestation. If we
have the strength not to react to these manifestations, they
cease. On the other hand, there are actual deficiencies in our
experiences of outer life owing perhaps to fixed attitudes that
limit the scope of our interests and abilities. It is important to
realise that it is not so much the nature of a task that renders it
inferior or superior as the imaginary value we put on it ourselves. For the balanced man there is a time for washing the
kitchen floor and a time for, say, composing an opera. Cer-
tainly we are not ready for the second education if we have
done little to apply the disciplines taught in the first, which
had the ultimate object of teaching us to discipline ourselves.
In our school days we often felt resentment towards the masters or mistresses who imposed discipline upon us and we regarded discipline simply as a force that thwarted our freedom.
Now we need to see discipline differently, as the strength of the
essential desire holding us to the aim of dying to every imaginary feeling of 'I'. Its purpose is to ensure that as being gradually opens to the spirit, which may be compared to a supremely
powerful electric current, it can receive its radiations. Without preparation the darkness of self-ignorance cannot receive
any enlightenment at all. The light of self-knowledge is indeed
a shock and without such shocks we would continue to repeat
the mechanical pattern of our lives. If this is understood we
may now be able to cancel any resentment we still feel towards
our schoolmasters and mistresses, for there is no one but our-

selves to command our wayward wills to keep an aim and see that it is carried out.

Another difficulty that may beset us concerns the idea of authority because, again from school days, we associate authority with discipline as an outward force. However, real authority is best illustrated by the parable of the centurion whose servant was sick and who besought Jesus to save him. The key words are, 'But say the word and my servant shall be healed. For I also am a man set under authority, having under myself soldiers: and I say unto this one, Go, and he goeth; and to another, Come, and he cometh, and to my servant, Do this, and he doeth it. And when Jesus heard these things, he marvelled at him, and turned and said unto the multitude that followed him, I say unto you, I have not found so great faith, no, not in Israel.'

From this parable it can be seen that both faith and authority are only understandable if higher and lower is a principle, that everything is a question of levels, and that a lower level must always obey a higher level. The authority we need to obey resides in our selves at a higher level and esoteric teachings prepare us to realise it. True authority manifests without any taint of self-feeling and hence without any projection of oneself upon another. 'It is connected with the power that a man may gain over himself, in the sense of making all that is in him, all his different desires, different momentary wills, different thoughts, moods, etc., obey something in him owing to the fact that this something in him is of such a nature that it deprives all these different things of any power to affect him' (Maurice Nicoll, *The New Man*, London,

1950). The 'something' in us is the real self that is always in us but awaits our conscious separation from all that we feel and imagine ourselves to be.

Jesus used the term 'My Father which is in Heaven' to describe the authority that he obeyed, but the sense-based mind has never understood that this signified the highest level of his own inner being. Only the experience of such a state gives understanding of it, but a parable can, for some people, convey a vision of it. Were all levels of our being to be in their rightful order, conducting harmony up and down the scale, authority would be in attendance.

*   *   *

Discipline and authority describe or symbolise qualities of being inherent in levels above self-emotions, and they are not realised before we have gained power over our selves, which would mean that our real self had been liberated from the domination of the personality and its imaginary self. There are many influences causing us to fear the idea of giving up self-emotions, even when faith is strong, for it is as if we were being asked to annihilate ourselves, so attached are we to the feeling of our own preciousness. The effect of this feeling is always to put our interests first, as does a mother identified with her child, and to expect everyone to 'mother' us. And making it even more difficult to gain power over ourselves, there is often an image that our parents, having failed to attain for themselves, impose on us, or, if we have been neglected of affection, orphaned, or solitary, there is the image of ourselves that we have invented. It seems hardly possible to avoid being an invented person and although we may have been taught to be considerate towards others and may seem to practise this, we do so only out of consideration for ourselves.

An enormous amount of energy is devoted to preserving and defending the image of what we wish other people to be persuaded that we are. Sometimes, for quite long periods, the image prevails, but when it fails to gain the response we desire we fall into moods of extreme depression, self-pity, resentment, or bitterness. If the image we have taken so much trouble to invent proves illusory, what is to become of us when the feeling of ourselves has been demolished? As quickly as possible we seek to restore our false equilibrium, usually by means of some distorted justification. As long as this pattern repeats itself, the essential self is imprisoned. All our psychic energy is being stolen and the seed of our essential self receives nothing to germinate it.

Without the shock that comes from seeing the meaninglessness of this invented self and without the faith that there is a real self to be found, we shall remain dominated by the negativeness of self-feeling. If, however, we have been fortunate enough to keep alive the sense of wonder that quickens the spirit, it will be easier to train and develop the intuitive and cognitive parts of the emotions that are concerned for meaning, good, and truth. Consequently, the memory of who we are and why we are on earth will be more readily revived when we begin to hear a teaching.

Within us there is a real conscience, defined as 'feeling all together', that knows, understands, and is all that has to be taught through the outer ears in esoteric schools. It is the heart of our essential being, yet as long as our centre of gravity is in the invented image, it is inaccessible. Ordinary, imaginary consciousness is unaware of it. The voice of real conscience speaks to us first from the outside, telling us how we may hear its internal utterances. The difference between a conscience that has been acquired and real conscience is that the latter is the same for everybody. There is a great variety in the nature of acquired consciences, depending upon upbringing, nationality, religion, gender, and contemporary bias. More often than not it infects our pride and vanity, so easily offended. Much of history is an account of crimes committed in the name of conscience—the Roman Catholic church's persecution of 'heretics', Protestants against Roman Catholics, the Crusades, Hindus versus Muslims, Arabs against Jews. There are innumerable examples, including men's restriction of women's rights. In one country a man may have several wives, in another he is prosecuted for bigamy if he has more than one; both are according to 'conscience' translated into law. 'Conscience' has been used to excuse the greed that has often been the motive for one country making war upon another. These examples are more than sufficient to illustrate the self-interested nature of the acquired conscience: it has no spiritual reality and therefore no power to transcend man's animal violence. As real conscience is the same for everybody it is the source of conscious relationship, a unifying, instead of a dividing, influence.

Were our first education to evoke the inherent talents of the emotions, we would more easily be able to withstand the violence of the untamed instincts, so prominent a feature of life. Lacking positive development, the emotions are frequently poisoned by the injured and offended self-feelings and infected by the negative condition of other people. In consequence, the negative part of the emotions plays the major role in our emotional life. 'Roughly speaking, as we are, it is central in us, particularly in regard to such inner life as we have . . . the impurity of our emotional states is due largely to pretence, to meritoriousness, to falseness, to all sorts of forms of showing off, to self-deception and insincerity. We have a quite wrong sense of ourselves, believing in our merit, believing that we can do good from ourselves, that we are conscious, that we have Will, and so on' (Maurice Nicoll, *Psychological Commentaries on the Teaching of G. I. Gurdjieff and P. D. Ouspensky*, London, 1952). Sometimes, when we see the enormous power of negative emotions governing us and the world in general, we feel we would do anything to be free of them, but nothing can be done while our centre of gravity is still in the invented self, for this both thinks and feels negatively by reason of its fictitiousness. If a person not entirely based on sensual thinking endeavours to think psychologically, 'sees that there are levels of meaning, that things are not necessarily opposites, on the same level, not antagonistic, but on different levels, he may perceive that scale is behind all things, if order is scale, and if to set in order is to set in scale then what is higher and what is lower must exist. But to think beyond the evidence of the senses is founded on faith which makes this possible. Without psychological thinking one is shut to the intuitions that only faith opens out to every mind that hitherto has been asleep in the senses and the limited world revealed by them' (*ibid.*). This way of thinking can lead on to seeing that our way of taking life is our life, and that it is the way of taking life, not life itself, that can be changed, if we manage to detach ourselves from the invented self.

Without the ability to perceive that there are levels of meaning, no one can understand esoteric ideas in such a way that they will undergo a transformation of being, because before any transformation can take place the manner of thinking must change. Sense-based thinking and the exaggerated respect for the intellect prevent · esoteric teaching from penetrating the emotions and affecting the will, with the consequence that none of their spermatic power is received. Our amazing technological inventiveness and knowledge, our administrative and organising skills, our scholarship and powers of analysis, *etcetera*, have all contributed to the general assumption that material evidence is the substance of 'real' life and that aesthetic, artistic, and spiritual concerns do not merit much acknowledgement because they are 'emotional'. Hence the blindness to the consequences of our actions, the insensibility to the inner, invisible feelings of other people, our deafness to real conscience, which are part of the causes of the sickness of the Western world and its imitators. If progress is seen only in terms of an increase in the quantity of material production and if the cognitive and evaluative powers of the emotions are regarded as irrelevant and derogatory, we cut ourselves off from 'the sense and significance of life on the earth in general and of human life in particular' (J. G. Bennett, *Gurdjieff: Making a New World*, London, Turnstone Books, 1973). In this way we deprive ourselves of essential meaning. However zealously we may have applied ourselves to our profession or occupation, however devoted we may have been, the meaning derived from it has come from an outside source and vanishes when the impulse that has driven us dies. What is left if there is no inner meaning, if the vital questions have never been asked?

Our *raison d'être* lies within us by reason of there being a self-existing higher authority, sometimes called 'God', not a figure of flesh and blood as presented by theologians, but our own inner highest state, which contains our spiritual forces. We begin towards their discovery when the sense of wonder urges us to seek meaning beyond the senses.

'When a man finds no Meaning in anything he has at the same time no feeling of God. Meaninglessness is a terrible illness. It has to be got over. It is the same as godlessness, because if you say there is no God you are saying that there is no meaning in things. But if you think there is Meaning, you believe in God. Meaning is God. You cannot say that you do not believe in God but believe that there is Meaning in things. The two are the same, in that one cannot be without the other. *God is Meaning*. If you dislike the word *God*, then say *Meaning* instead. The word God shuts some people's minds. The word Meaning cannot. It opens the mind.

'Meaning was before *Time* began. It was before creation,

for creation occurs in running Time, in which birth and death exist. Birth and death belong to the passage of Time. But Meaning was before Time and creation in Time began. There is no way of describing existence in the higher dimensional world outside Time, save by the language of passing Time—of past, present and future. Meaning *is*—not *was*—before the beginning of creation in Time. It does not belong to what is becoming and passing away but in what *is*, above Time. If, then, there is Meaning above our heads, what is our meaning by creation?' (Maurice Nicoll, *The Mark*, London, 1954).

The divorce between thought and emotion has starved the deepest and most real part of us. Society has taken the path of negation, evading all acts of understanding as sentimental, or as scientifically and commercially valueless. We live in a world of effects whose causes remain hidden. Our thinking is sense-based, the wrong way round. We think sense is prior to mind. Nothing internal can belong to us: the natural order is inverted. Ultimately everything is dealt with by violence. 'For the sensory object, taken as *ultimate* and highest reality, can be smashed, injured, blown up or killed. That is why materialism is so dangerous psychologically. It not only *closes* the mind and its possible ingiven development but turns everything the wrong way round, so much so that men seriously explain the house by its bricks, or the universe by its atoms and are content with explanations extraordinarily poor of this quality' *(ibid)*.

V. The Functions of Different Minds

CONTINUING to prepare ourselves to receive a teaching that, first of all, if we apply it, will harmonise and balance the five minds, it is important to study the quite wonderful functions and attributes of the instincts. Instinct has its own kind of intelligence, different from the intelligences of the emotions and of the brain. It is the one mind fully functioning when we are born.

'The Instinctive Centre attends to the inner working of the organism and is itself the representation of the organic life cosmos in Man, or what is ordinarily called nature. The cleverness of this centre is beyond all computation . . . Without this starting point man could not exist on the Earth. He is given this first of all and also a small development in Moving Centre' (Maurice Nicoll, *Psychological Commentaries on the Teaching of G. I. Gurdjieff and P. D. Ouspensky*, London, 1952).

If the intelligence of the instincts was interfered with the body would be under no direction. Yet perhaps because we are born with this intelligence fully functioning, it is difficult for us to take ourselves as anything but the body. 'When we take ourselves as our bodies we get a wrong impression. This impression, acting as a cause, produces as an effect the idea that we are nothing but our bodies. . . . If we begin to get another impression of ourselves the idea that we are *not* only our bodies

41

may replace the former idea. The replacement of the former idea by the latter idea is important. Actually it is of the greatest importance in regard to anyone's psychological development. . . . It is extraordinary and only realisable very gradually how we cling to this physical concept of ourselves. . . . But even our own bodies can seem strange and incongruous at times—these fingers, nails, teeth, this hair, nose, mouth, this head, this wart—so much so that for a flash you may sometimes wonder if it really is you' (*ibid.*).

Apart from the effects that instincts have upon the feeling of ourselves, they possess attributes such as taste, sensation, the apprehension of physical danger and protection from it. 'When fear is stimulated by the sensory impression of danger it excites a secretion from the adrenalin glands and releases material that activates the muscles, either for attack or defence' (*ibid.*). If the feeling of ourselves derives from identification with the body, we will always be suspicious of others, like dogs sniffing at each other and suddenly breaking into violent attack, or just as suddenly taking an instant liking to one another. As long as we ascribe our lives to ourselves and know only self-emotions, we are bound to have many fears and suspicions of others, which may give way to violence.

The intelligence that controls and directs the body's organism, upon which our physical well-being depends, is greater than perhaps we ever attain in the brain and in the emotions. We do not know how this intelligence came to be, nor can we create it; it is a gift. It has other properties, such as a sense for making things, for arranging details in the right order for something to manifest, as in joinery and carpentry, making bread, making wine, the art and craft of husbandry—sowing seeds, planting, breeding cattle, sheep, chickens, ducks, the health of the soil. With training, these senses can become skills. Instinct has a sense of direction that helps us to find our way across unfamiliar country, chooses foods suitable for our bodies if some theory has not interfered with its knowledge, and delights in the culinary arts when taught how to practise them. There is animal love, the sheer physical sensation a mother has for her baby, and animal rage, the desire to kill when, for instance, jealousy overpowers us to the exclusion of all else. If the instincts are not trained, they may exert their natural power over us to such a degree that intellectual and emotional development is inhibited, or they may themselves be inhibited from functioning well by some acquired attitude in the intellectual or emotional minds. For example, although there are certain signs indicating when fruit is ripe and when mushrooms are edible, it is instinct with its memory of sensations and associations that guides our decision to pick, or not to pick, and eat—provided that commercial reasons do not enter into the question.

Intermeshed with the mind of the instincts is the mind governing movements, both having control over the body. The miraculous control of limbs, hands, and fingers through the muscular system can be studied in its mechanics, but the instantaneous working of the mind of Moving Centre surpasses the speed with which the intellectual mind functions. Although limbs can move, we have to be taught to walk, but the muscles used for breathing, digestion and excretion are working at birth. Our breathing by means of contracting and relaxing muscles is controlled by 'Instinctive Centre', which estimates the condition of the blood at every moment and increases or decreases the rate of respiration accordingly.

Both instincts and movements have minds that remember. In Moving Centre 'lie all kinds of extraordinary memories, memory for walking, for skating, for writing, for speaking, for balancing, for bicycling, for eating, for sewing, for knitting, for doing everything with your hands and with your feet. . . . In Instinctive Centre lie memories of sensations. . . . When you are eating something that gives you a particular sensation of taste, smell, consistency, you are reminded of other similar sensations by association. This is memory of sensations. Or when you eat a thing said to be lamb and it is not, you know it is not. Sensation works in the present moment only, just as all the senses do' (ibid.).

Everyone who enjoys watching good acting on the stage recognises that the posture and movement of an actor or actress convey the inner thoughts and feelings of the character they are portraying and complement the dialogue. If the face expresses delight or gloom, for example, the body adopts a corresponding posture, and we know what he or she is undergoing. In fact, every posture and every expression denote the inner state of the character being portrayed. This remark may be taken as a glimpse of the obvious, since such is the technique of acting, but does it occur to us that our bodies mechanically assume postures, and the face expressions, corre-

sponding to every change of mood? Are we aware that there
are muscular habits in our movements of body and face that,
occurring mechanically, induce, mechanically, pleasant and
unpleasant moods, and other habits that conjure interesting, or
trivial, or negative, or profound thoughts? When these habits
of the muscles are observed we begin to understand how strongly our psychology is governed by the body, causing our consciousness to remain asleep.

Of all the minds acting upon the body, that of sex has the
fastest speed of reaction to stimulae. Oblivious that we are psychologically asleep, we now imagine that we are more sincere
towards sex than were previous generations and that we have
arrived at this sincerity by some sort of evolutionary progress.
Since we are not psychologically awake, it is more probable
that our change of attitude has been caused by a natural force,
such as that exerted by the planets, without our having any
choice in the question. In any case, we are each conditioned
by the quality of our sexual energy. This influences the nature
of our sexual life, which imposes itself upon our thoughts and
emotions as well as itself being influenced by them.

It is usual to take sex as a physical force only, but certain
esoteric teachings indicate how it may be transformed into an
energy that helps to awaken consciousness; for instance, it has
been said that man's aim should be regeneration, and not generation. The ideas of Robert Fludd, an English mystic of the sev-
enteenth century, can help us to understand the meaning of this
aim and how sexual energy can connect us with a higher level
of consciousness—the original intention of celibacy for the

45

priesthood. In a work dealing with the inner nature of man, entitled *Utriusque Cosmi*, Fludd refers to two psychological systems, upon which Dr Maurice Nicoll comments as follows in *Living Time* (London, 1952): 'Let us look at a diagram made by Fludd. . . . Here are two triangles which represent something in man's constitution. In one the apex is downwards, in the other upwards. We are at once reminded of the double triangles in the hieroglyph called the Seal of Solomon, representing the three dimensions of space and the three dimensions of "time" according to Ouspensky.

'As regards the triangle with the base downwards Fludd (in another diagram) divides it from below into *body, vital spirits* and *reason*. The reason touches the base of the upper triangle at a point in the level which Fludd denotes as *mind, i.e.,* the highest use of man's ordinary reason touches the level of mind (mens). It is, however, merely a *point* in "mind". The upper triangle terminates in man's *sex* as a point. We might say, then, that there is a point in man's reason and a point in man's sex that connects him with a level of consciousness on a higher scale than on his ordinary one. . . . But it would be better to say that the two *systems* of consciousness are represented by the two overlying triangles. . . . The triangle with its base upwards, ending below at the point on the level of sex, is related to the three time dimensions of the "invisible world". When consciousness is situated in this system the sense of the life extended in Time, the sense of eternity and recurrence, and the sense of self-existence, may all appear. They belong to the higher system which is concealed in man. When man is in his natural state he is in the psychological system represented by the triangle with the base downwards. So if we study "natural" man we will find only this system in him. But, psychologically considered, man cannot be taken in terms only of one system. Some extraordinary *paradox* exists within his being. Another system is latent in him whose mode of action is in a reversed direction to the natural system. If we are willing to follow this interpretation it means that *fully integrated* man must be some combination of these two systems. . . . They represent a paradox, a cross, something extremely difficult to bring into union—above all something which must be roused into activity, because "natural" man is adequate to life and need not know the action of the second system. The task is to *bring these two systems into relationship*—not to seek one at the expense of the other.'

What is striking in this commentary on Fludd is the idea that there is a point in man's reason and a point in man's sex that connect him with a level of consciousness on a higher scale than his ordinary one: that reason and sex, if connected by an aim relating both, would increase consciousness: that there are a natural system and a latent psychological system. Someone who perceives that evolution requires his own growth of consciousness, or who, putting it another way, realises his need to become conscious at a higher level than his ordinary level, may be able to recognise that sexual energy, combined with other energies, if so directed, can become a means of regeneration.

47

But to be able to accept this and to practise it, a considerable degree of maturity and balance are requisite. First, however, the 'natural' system needs to be physically healthy and free from perversions and phantasies. It is from a man's feminine side that his inner evolution grows, and it is from a woman's masculine side that her inner evolution grows. If for some reason these inner attributes have become externalised, such as, for instance, imitation of the opposite sex used as a function for dealing with external life, inner development is blocked. What is more, our essence which, before it evolves, is our weakest element, is being mortally wounded. Again, if we are content to remain without activating the psychological system latent within ourselves, our sexual condition is limited to the 'natural' alone, unconnected with a higher level of consciousness.

The ideas of Fludd suggest that by bringing the two systems together our inward masculine and feminine sides may be united; that by redirecting the expression of the powerful energy necessary for experiencing higher levels of consciousness, the natural and the psychological man can be integrated. This indeed requires a different goal than that of self-love, which demands as its main object a favourable reflection of ourselves in others. Only the recognition that there are higher degrees of reality, and the emotions that such a recognition can rouse, can begin to give the right starting point. For such emotions do not lie in the sphere of self-love. Therefore a profound understanding of the aim and the good of conserving and directing sexual energy is required first, which may begin when we have a glimmering that love of another person depends upon an actual development of consciousness, in order to feel their real, objective existence.

VI. Love and Real Conscience

ON the long inner path from self-love to 'Love of God', the highest order of reality, we start with our ordinary idea of love, and even with the imagination that we are able to love, turned towards physical people and objects. We do not understand what it is to love beyond ourselves. Lacking a permanent, unchanging 'I', what is called a real 'I', and being a multitude of changing 'I's, we know only the feeling of the changing emotions. Unless, among the variety of emotions passing through us, there is the will to find a way of attaining a permanent self, we shall remain a creature of the self-love. Conscious love is the attribute of unified consciousness, defined as 'knowing all together', and of nothing less. It is this unified consciousness, what is called 'Love of God', that is the *realisation* in ourselves of the unity of all life. Without the faith that such a level of being exists, we have nothing in us strong enough to surpass self-love.

* * *

Practical common sense is needed in applying a teaching to our being. For a long time our valuation of a teaching is mixed with various other valuations: we love ourselves, we are full of self-merit, pride, and vanity. Unless valuation of a teaching begins to be winnowed from these, we shall not work on ourselves and consequently will understand nothing. When a separation of values begins it becomes possible to discriminate between them and to see that even the teaching is, instead of diminishing, increasing the feeling of self-merit. All teachings exist to help us realise that within us lies buried a self that is not an imitation, but true to its own being, and in this sense, that there is something bigger and higher than ourselves as we are now. Each teaching has its own manner of expressing this idea, and on first hearing our self-love may tend, in its usual way, to feel flattered. This will continue until some insight brings us to question the quality of our valuation of the teaching and of ourselves, and to the admission that self-love is valued the greater. No change in the level of our being occurs before there is a change in the quality of the love.

When a few 'I's in the personality begin to feel the influence of a teaching and are, momentarily at least, free from the mass of self-regarding, self-interested, self-loving 'I's', there is then someone within ourselves who can begin to evaluate the teaching. Yet we can take an intellectual interest in a teaching, which is only temporary because the emotions fail to be engaged. Consequently, as there is no will to practise it, there is nothing to hold the attention of the intellect for long. It is necessary by means of uncritical, objective insight to become aware of the conflicting emotions and values. If the will is to be affected by a teaching strongly enough to bring about the attempt to practise it in daily life, the struggle to separate from the self-emotions has to be undertaken by those few 'I's' that, to begin with, feel its influence. The will remains weak until further 'I's' in the emotions combine together to respond to the ideas being registered and recorded in the intellect, always provided that we reflect on them and try to understand them for ourselves. It is the understanding that provides the force energising the will when, in turn, the truth of an idea illumines the mind. Nevertheless, the multifarious illusions of ourselves, such as that we are conscious and always the same person, begin to be offended as the light of the teaching begins to show them up. Gradually we verify for ourselves that what Western psychology calls consciousness is a very dangerous state of sleep in which millions of people kill millions of others, feeling themselves fully conscious: 'The level of consciousness below it, sleep in bed, is harmless in comparison. We do not, while we are in bed, go and kill one another in the name of liberty and justice and patriotism, but in the so-called waking state of consciousness. . . . all the evil events of the world take place' (Maurice Nicoll, *Psychological Commentaries, etc.* London, 1952). Our ordinary state of consciousness, the so-called waking state, is characterised by barriers that prevent one 'I' from being aware of another and thus prevent us from seeing what we are really doing and saying, and the harm being caused, 'so that we can do the most contradictory things without pain to ourselves, aided by the accessory capacity we have of justifying ourselves in everything we say and do, so that this state of sleep we call consciousness is intensified' (*ibid.*). Perhaps, therefore, the first important shock to awaken us to our complacency and self-imagination comes when we see the discrepancy between a certain idea of ourselves and what we really are. The illusion of being conscious is then no longer quite so strong: the imaginary self has a little less predominance over our psychology, real conscience is less inaccessible. This shock may also help to bring us to realise that we live in the hypnotic sleep of the imaginary, 'invented' self. Yet because it has been our habit to live in the so-called waking state we cannot remain awake after merely one shock; an endless succession of shocks are needed to awaken the sleeper. Many of these are given at the right psychological time by a teacher, some occur when we have a moment of new insight into ourselves; eventually we have to be aware when it is necessary to give ourselves a shock and to be able to assess the means by which it will be effectively applied, for there comes a day when we have to bear the burden of ourselves without support from a teacher.

However well-trained is the intellect, however efficient and healthy is the physical body, its instincts, and its sexual energy, it is the emotions that are the key to inner evolution and to the quality of the application to our psychological being of the methods presented by a teaching. The emotions, if not retarded, have the wonderful talents of intuition, clairvoyance, and cognition, but, on the other hand, are terribly subject to the poison of negativeness, the worst kind of infection that is transmitted from generation to generation. As long as the feeling of ourselves is concentrated in the fictitious self, how can we expect to be free of negative emotions? Quite unconsciously, we squander an intense amount of energy in trying to sustain the customary feeling of ourselves. Before there is any possibility of transforming our being, we have to become aware of this wastage and of its many causes, gradually detaching ourselves from them. This will begin to conserve the energy necessary for psychological evolution. The more we observe the personality, the more aware we become of the emotion sustaining the illusion of reality in each 'I', and that this emotion has a strong self-will that always seeks its own interest. These numerous self-wills, determined to preserve their realms, resist any other good but their own. They constitute a formidable opposition to the good that the teaching can evoke from real conscience. People who are so well proofed against awareness of their contrary sides and whose emotions will not admit that they are asleep neither wish to nor are able to receive a teaching.

Our most difficult task is to purify ourselves of negative emotions, the poison that governs the world. They are destructive of the evolutionary seed within us and have a baleful attraction for humanity. Unfortunately we are all sure that we, at least, are not negative, and consequently it is with reluctance that we direct our attention towards this feature that we justify for a long time, so loath are we to admit that we have identified with it. Once we see how much psychic energy is lost through indulging negative emotions, we begin to realize how important it is to endeavour not to fall into this trap.

The aim of a teaching is to awaken us from our sense-based, psychological sleep, so that we realise that we are not conscious, from the point of view of esoteric psychology. Then it may become possible for us to die to every supposition of ourselves. If this psychological death occurs we may become 'The New Man', or 'The Second Born'. While we are riddled with negative emotions this inner evolution cannot proceed, for the energy that is needed is being stolen by them.

Until we begin to understand the good of the truth that we are being taught, we shall not know what a positive emotion really is. Self-emotions mechanically swing between opposites, but a positive emotion does not change at all. For a moment we may know what it is like to be freed from ourselves. Such an experience brings a new state of being, one that gives a taste of an altogether different kind of life; instead of being acted upon by every kind of event and by every kind of thought and emotion, we are free of the usual reactions and can see the incommensurable difference between being under the power of the personality and being in command of it. We can realise what it means that we do *not have* to react. Such is the quality of a positive emotion when the good is understood: it actually conducts a far finer psychic energy than anything previously experienced, and it is this energy that vivifies a level of consciousness hitherto latent.

But the overcoming, or rather, the transcending, of negative emotions is a major task; it may be likened to a battle in the heart such as is dramatised in *The Bhagavad-Gita, The Songs of the Master, Krishna*. Krishna instructs his pupil, Arjuna—that is, oneself—in how to contend with life and our reactions to it. We have to become aware that every idea, every thought, every feeling, every supposition about every person and every event of life proceed from our own invention and are projected upon the outside scene. Unconsciously we ask the universe to respond to what we request from it: hence our life. It corresponds to the nature of the requests. If we wish to know why we are having a certain kind of life, we need to become aware of these unconscious requests. If we wish for a life that is not prone to chance and accident, we need to learn how not to be identified with these unconscious requests. As Christ said, a man's foes are those in his own household, which he symbolised as influences called 'father', 'mother', 'brother', 'sister'. It is for each of us to discover the meaning of these symbols.

In everyone, whether it be symbolised by the name Krishna, or Christ, or Buddha, there are, on a level of being and consciousness unknown to the psychology of the natural system, a fully developed intellectual mind and a fully developed emotional mind. Were we to gain access to these two higher minds, our lives would be directed in conformity with the evolution of essence; that is to say, we would know exactly what is the task constituting each stage of self-development and how to meet it. Our attention is directed to these minds and their qualities in allegorical literature. Scriptures such as the Bible's parable and miracles of Christ, the Eightfold Path of Buddhism, the awakening of the Bodhi mind in Milarepa's song to Dharma Bodhi of Nepal, the Hindu concept of Atman, Brahman, the Sufi 'Lover' and 'Beloved', all tell us what we are, what is already created within us, but which is unrealisable as long as we are unready to receive, unable to be *en rapport* with, these two fully developed higher minds. In order to hear these two higher minds, the five minds of the mechanical, natural man must be transcended by a development of the consciousness.

VII. Transformation
of Being

FROM our being merely a physical body with a personality, from taking ourselves as one, believing that that which thinks, speaks, acts, feels, loves, and hates is always one and the same, it is possible, by an inner development of individuality, consciousness, and will, to cease to be a machine driven by outer circumstances. Then we would have something organised in us that could resist life, something from which we could act. The starting point of this inner organisation is the dividing of ourselves into an observing and an observed side. Unless this division begins, unless we can become the subject of our own observations, nothing will ever develop in us that can eventually control us inwardly and make the outer machine obey. 'But a man who has begun to have something internally organised in him is no longer so easily driven by outer life but is at times controlled from something within himself' (*ibid.*).

The real part of us is Essence: we are born as Essence, but it is very small, primitive, and undeveloped. Through our contact with life—parents, teachers, our whole upbringing—Essence is surrounded by Personality. Personality grows but does not make Essence grow: on the contrary, it imprisons Essence and controls the inner life, assisted by the immense power of imagination which persuades us that we are real people. There does, indeed, exist a 'Real I' that can be reached by means of the development of consciousness, beginning when we succeed in

59

dividing ourselves into observing and observed sides. Our aim, therefore, is to help Essence to evolve. Paradoxically 'Real I' is not some kind of superego; it is consciousness purified from every feeling of 'I' because it is at-one-ment: its knowledge and its being are each fully developed, it has Will, it can do what it knows.

Our state of sleep, our mechanicalness, is characterised by the reactions of the personality that we mistake for activity, and the passivity of Essence. This relationship between Personality and Essence is maintained by the hypnotic, driving force of life, and it can be changed only by a force coming from the influences transmitted through the lineage of those who have themselves attained enlightenment. We have to learn how to receive these influences in order to fertilise our essence, so that the part of us that is not belonging to organic life but which hitherto is subject to its laws may rightfully evolve. We exchange worn-out meanings for new meanings, if we are capable of receiving influences that can, by means of our own long inner struggle, render personality passive and essence active.

The process of essential growth, the long inner struggle, lasts a lifetime because we start without the power to be mindful of our presence in the present moment; we have not the ability to concentrate, direct, and hold attention psychologically. Consequently, the memory of ourselves is lacking until we have been trained in how to form and evoke this memory. Even then we keep forgetting to apply the methods, taught in various ways by various teachings, that bring about awareness of the present moment. Always we are anywhere but in the present. Our consciousness is divided, our sense of ourselves changes with every changing thought and mood. If we are to be masters of ourselves, we have to become unified in consciousness and in will.

Mostly we live waiting for our attention to be attracted by something interesting enough to animate one or another of the multifarious persons inhabiting us. That is to say, without realising it, we rely on energy coming from outside to animate us. But it is only the Personality that is energised. Nothing external, unless consciously transformed, gives Essence the energy to grow. Waiting upon external stimulae is characteristic of Personality, but under such conditions Essence remains passive.

Our task is to discover how to remove the imposing domination of Personality upon Essence, so that essence, the latent oak tree within the acorn, may receive the right nourishment to provide the energy for its evolution. This task requires an especially strong evaluation and understanding of the idea that we are created with the possibility of living on a level of being that is free from sense-based influences when consciousness replaces ingrained reactions to them, if we are to practice the requisite discipline, which of course is voluntary. We shall quickly discover that it is the inability to direct attention that enfeebles our practice, so that most of us have to train ourselves to concentrate and direct attention, which also means discovering what distracts attention. First of all, this training is an exercise of the formatory mind; later it becomes willed by delight when its good is perceived. This is an experience that comes when something is seen or heard and related to by means of directed attention: our consciousness receives impressions that are objective, instead of the usual subjective response from ingrained associations and mechanical reactions. Thus, an event, an idea, a familiar experience, are seen in an entirely new light, as they actually are, because we are not projecting ourselves upon them. Now we can begin to understand that we never see the real nature of any person, let alone the nature of ourselves and the nature of the phenomenal world, because in between reality and ourselves are interposed all the attitudes and imagination acquired with the formation of personality. We are related to events by attitudes, and it is through attitudes that we associate an event as pleasant or unpleasant. Indifference to an event simply signifies the absence of an attitude. When an event, an idea, a familiar experience, are seen as they actually are, free from the projections of the minds, they are neither good nor bad but neutral. Indeed, as *The Tibetan Book of the Dead* teaches, the world we see through the senses is a projection of our imagination.

When we begin to awaken, even a little, and look upon our lives, we ask ourselves if hitherto we have been insane, if we have not been in a dream. We can see that almost everything composing our lives has occurred without our conscious direction. Upon meeting a teaching we bring with us all our habits of thinking, habits of emotions, habits of instincts, habits of physical movements, without realising that all have been acquired and become fixed through constant repetition. Our life is a reaction, from these acquired habits, to outer events and inner states. We have no consciousness, no individuality and no will, but we are, for the most part, beginning to wonder if we are masters of ourselves, if any habit with its concomitant feeling of 'I' is our real self. An enormous amount of physical and psychological energy is wasted by involuntary reactions, but on becoming aware of this whole process it begins to be possible to withdraw the feeling of 'I' from a habitual reaction, and thus save a modicum of energy. Without conscious energy 'Real I' cannot be animated, therefore we have to become aware of how our energy is lost, then learn how to prevent its loss and eventually how to make energy. Essence—the seed of our Real Self, the nucleus of consciousness, individuality, and Will, the meaning of our creation as an experiment in self-development—cannot evolve without the ordinary energy supplied by nature being transformed into a superfine psychic substance.

The transformation of our being from a state of psychological sleep into psychological consciousness has to begin by our minds being taught new ideas from which to think about ourselves, about other people, and about the things of life. These give us knowledge of the possible inner evolution, knowledge that is a map of the way to inner evolution. But no amount of knowledge makes evolution. Until we use this knowledge in the way a teaching instructs, it makes no difference to our being; no development occurs; we can even become more asleep. Unless the good in the knowledge is felt, there is no will to practice it, and its truth is neither proved nor disproved; we lack the new meaning that would help to provide the force for our transformation. When, through applying the teaching, the meaning of the knowledge begins to become alive, when we feel the good of its truth, when through insight our understanding has an emotional force, then transformation starts.

Do not study a teaching to learn about the teaching; study a teaching to learn about yourself.

VIII. Summary

IF you are accepted as a pupil in an esoteric school you may feel so enthused that your impulse is to tell your friends and family about it, indiscriminately, and especially to proclaim that everybody is unconsciously asleep. You should abstain from this impulse, as it will be met, for the most part, with a disdainful scepticism and you will be asked for logical proof that mankind is asleep. Realise that as yet you are merely parroting one of the ideas you have been told; you have not understood that it applies to yourself; you have not become aware that you yourself are asleep. Consequently the idea that mankind is asleep, as knowledge, inflates your sense of superiority; but you are quite incapable of convincing the sceptical mentality of people whose minds are sense-based, limited to the logical level. It is a mistake to give way to initial enthusiasm indiscriminately; your own inability to give logical proof of a psychological idea may make you doubt the truth of it and the whole good of the teaching you are being given.

Sooner or later someone will charge you with being very self-centred not to help other people before seeking your own salvation. We are all self-centred and it is exactly in showing us what we are like that all esoteric teaching affects us. It gradually removes self-centredness; it goes against selfishness and self-complacency, self-esteem and phantasies about oneself. It makes you see that you have to do something about yourself before you can even try to help other people.

'How can you help other people unless you have become

65

more conscious of yourself? How can the blind lead the blind? Before you start off helping other people for heaven's sake look at yourself and see whether you can really help yourself to begin with. Do you call this self-satisfied imposing your self-will on other people helping them? . . . according to the degree that the Work has changed you in yourself your help will be valuable. . . . Thinking you can help other people as you are means simply that you impose your ideas of what other people should be on them without realising what you are like yourself. . . . The less blind you are to yourself the more you can help people who are still blind to themselves, but to become less blind to oneself takes many years of hard work and much pain and much overcoming of self-will, self-love, and much overcoming of prejudices, of thinking that you know everything . . . this Work does not begin with what we imagine we are. The world is full of False Personalities and each False Personality thinks he or she knows best. The Work . . . gradually drains away from us all these imaginings and falsities about ourselves. Then perhaps we can begin to help other people' (*ibid.*).

If the first reaction from your friends is hostile recognise that you are having your first experience of the difference in the level of being between those people who have psychological minds and those who have only logical thinking. Only people in whom the capacity for psychological thinking has been developed, due to their believing in 'Greater Mind', or 'God', are open to receive esoteric ideas. Therefore, do not speak about esoteric school ideas before you have verified at least one of the truths you are being taught so that to a certain degree you understand it, and are able to perceive whether or not people to whom you propose to speak believe in something higher than themselves. Logical thinking crucifies psychological, 'spiritual', ideas. The psychological mind is able to perceive levels of being, of ideas, of qualities, of intelligence; the logical mind sees everything on one level and hence argues in terms of 'yes' or 'no': the psychological mind, being able to perceive levels, does not argue in terms of opposites, it includes 'yes' *and* 'no'.

This first reaction to your joining a school, on the part of those not belonging to it, can show you something of the element that qualifies our possible evolution from man asleep to man awake, namely our being. No natural development of our being, such as the growth of the body, takes place and the quality of being with which we are born stays the same unless it is influenced by forces derived from its own innate superior possibilities. It is not every being that is susceptible to the inner evolutionary powers: it has to have reached a certain level of preparation before it can be nourished and transformed further, in conscious co-operation with a teaching about man's possible inner evolution. The level of preparation is sometimes designated as a 'good householder'—someone who does his duties in life, meets his responsibilities, does not believe in life but continues to observe these standards—with 'magnetic centre', the ability to distinguish and experience influences coming from outside life which give the conviction that his true *raison d'être* can be realised only through their aid. It has always been the task of esoteric schools to convey their evolutionary ideas to those who wish and are ready to undertake the process

of inner, essential development. In turn, authentic schools receive their guidance from those who have attained to com-
pletion, or 'perfection', sometimes called *Shambhala*, sometimes
called the *Conscious Circle of Humanity*. But for the influence
of their ideas sown into humanity the influences of violent
nature would have predominated over mankind. Being free
from all violence they do not compel man to believe in anything beyond the evidence of the senses. They are efficacious
only if applied in voluntary and conscious willingness. As we
apply them to our being the voice of our real conscience makes
itself heard and we recognise in the teaching that what we hear
with our outer ears is the same as we are beginning to hear in
our inner ears. This is the dawn of our realisation that we are
born with all the faculties of evolution within us and the
memory of them, hitherto dormant, is now becoming acces-
sible. Awakening from the sleep of the senses, hypnotised by
life, depends upon an increase of consciousness so as to remember this essential memory more frequently and more profoundly. Once upon a time man remembered himself; but now that
the level of man has become so influenced by the forces playing
upon his personality that he has forgotten his essential memory
he can only be reminded of his true destiny by listening to and
endeavouring to apply the directions given by an esoteric
teaching which, throughout man's history, has preserved the
knowledge of psychological consciousness.

This knowledge includes a cosmological understanding of
the universe and man's place therein. It explains that we live
in a world of energies and levels of densities, a scale of

manifestation. Each manifestation takes its place on the scale according to the density of forces playing upon it, so that order is preserved, from highest to lowest, from the most conscious to the least conscious. The organic life covering the earth, of which man is a part, is influenced directly by the levels of energies above it, including the sun and the planets, and by the influence of the moon beneath it. Were man not to possess, as his birthright, the possibility of self-development, he would forever remain part of organic life serving nature. However, there are certain forces in the universe, which he can be taught to receive, that enable his being to be transformed and refined to a degree of excellence that he no longer has to serve nature. This knowledge has to be digested and understood, so that the latent microcosmos within ourselves is realised.

It is one thing to acquire new knowledge; but for it to become spermatic it has to become active in the depth of the understanding, and to gain this understanding continuous effort to apply it to our being is necessary. It is a test of our evaluation and sincerity. Without evaluation there is no reason or will to apply the knowledge and without application there is no understanding; the knowledge rests alongside all the other facts acquired in the first education, on the same level, causing more inflation of our already imaginary picture of ourselves. The knowledge remains superficial unless the intellect, in its emotional part, is genuinely stirred to discover its meaning. If this is the case a response is evoked from the part of the emotions themselves that may feel real conscience. Then there is a degree of real Will to apply what we know to our being, for we value nothing if it has no importance to ourselves. When real conscience begins to become active what was hitherto of importance to the imaginary self and its self-love decreases and gradually we begin to perceive that we have always neglected the realisation of the real self, from sheer ignorance of its existence.

Once it is perceived that there is a scale of values in which responsibility to essence must take the highest place the real struggle to relinquish self-love, vanity, and pride, all the attributes of the false personality, all its interests, all its ambitions, either starts or is abandoned. The question of values, so closely linked with consciousness of them, is the determining factor in the transformation of being. That is to say, whether attachment to all that is inessential is, or is not, more powerful than valuation and comprehension of essential being. Although our aim may be to achieve the development of essence in full consciousness, when we are aware of choice all the habitual feelings of ourselves assert themselves in resistance. If it is not already too late, pray for help to 'Heaven' within you that you may succeed in crossing the Rubicon, by conscious, willing effort.

Before coming to this inner, spiritual crisis it may have been assumed that esoteric knowledge is an addition to our knowledge, that we could stay the same and increase the sameness, despite ideas such as the necessity of 'dying to ourselves'. Yet if there is valuation of the ideas, eventually, by attempting to apply them, over a long period, it is realised that staying the same and undergoing transformation of being are mutually incompatible. It can thus be said that if there is real valuation there is the will to apply the ideas to our being, and if they are applied we begin to become aware of the factors hindering development. If, or as, efforts are made to surmount these factors, which *appear* to have become stronger once recognised, the force energising our efforts diminishes, vide the law of entropy. To reinforce and re-charge effort, return to a new and deeper evaluation of the chief aim of the teaching. With the experience now gained from first contending with yourself you will the better understand what effort on your own part is required in order to transcend all the habits of mind, habits of emotions, of instincts and of the body, and with this understanding can come a deeper and stronger evaluation. Each time that you arrive at a stage where factors in the personality and false personality seem to be intransigeant re-value the teaching, your motives and your understanding, in order to feel the renewal of force for the continuation of working on yourself. The more self-knowledge we gain the more we are able to differentiate between the side made by life's influences and the animation of the essential being which, without the nourishment of consciousness, remains dormant. Knowledge of the self is knowledge obtained from conscious, objective observation of the personality and the false personality. Observation effects a division between these acquired characteristics and the essential self. By withdrawing the feeling of self from what is observed the force which animates these multiple 'I's' is conserved for the enhancement of

71

Essence. In this way the real self makes itself known and the predominant power of all the influences that prevented this revelation is diminished.

While living in a state of sleep we are mostly inattentive, that is, we are unaware of what we are doing, of where we are, of what we are feeling, of bodily posture and movement. Ocassionally our attention is attracted by something that, fortuitously, interests some part of us; more rarely we actually concentrate and direct our attention upon a task, a problem, an aim. These three levels of attention characterise our mechanical life. We possess the ability to direct attention upon things exterior to ourselves and to the degree that we exercise it we are less under the hypnotic power of the forces of nature. We also possess the psychological ability to direct attention upon the states of our inner self, provided that there is sufficient concentration of energy. This depends upon having an aim to be aware of the 'I' and its state with which we are identified, in order to observe it and separate from it. Attention, like every other activity, requires energy, and the concentration of inner attention is the first indispensable act towards recollecting our self. Unless attention has been concentrated it is impossible to be aware that we can be conscious of and not identified with the 'I' of the moment. The aim to contain and conserve the energy that concentration of inner attention demands depends upon evaluation of the whole teaching. When this is forgotten, or when it is feeble, there is no aim: once more the personality and the false personality are mechanically active. Lack of aim always results in a relapse. It is therefore important to become aware of how energy is being lost; for example, a ceaseless flow of mindless chatter is the commonest cause. When this is seen and recorded in the memory of the observer we have the aim, every time this tendency repeats itself, to withdraw the intense feeling of ourselves from the mechanical 'I' that chatters. Whatever the cause of loss of energy the aim is the same, namely, to stop the leakages which are mostly in those of our activities which occur in the total absence of attention, but above all when we are identified with negative emotions.

Clearly, therefore, the foundation of all work on ourselves depends upon the quality of evaluation. Why should we undertake a task voluntarily in addition to the tasks that outer life thrusts upon us? If there is no exceptionally strong reason we avoid such a task. If we perceive that no matter what we have achieved, or hope to achieve, in life the real reason for our birth is not accomplished but awaits the development of Essence, then we may understand why nothing external to ourselves will be of aid. Should this profoundly affect the part of the emotions that can feel worth and value there will be a reason why we should wish to become conscious of the meaning of our birth. It may strike us that only a development of Essence by our own efforts can give the answer. Therefore we must apply the teaching to our being in order to transform it. It is not the logic of the intellect which decided this question, but the logic of the emotions expressing itself in real conscience.

The application of a teaching to our being is the process by which it is purified of the thousand and one mechanical reactions that govern our thoughts and our feelings and cause us to believe in an imaginary self despite its ever changing disunity. Whatever the method taught in our training it remains theoretical until, in every circumstance, it is willed and lived. It is only too usual for theory to supplant application, and unless we become aware of this our self-conceitedness and sense of superiority swell. Esoteric knowledge either awakens us or hypnotises us. If it is not valued, applied, and its truth experienced it endangers the being. For being uses knowledge according to its level and if that level is untransformed esoteric knowledge adds to, instead of diminishes, the false personality. So if purification of being from the imaginary self is not undertaken we shall not be able to receive aid from the interior influences of higher consciousness that are the attributes of the real self. As always, it is the quality of the evaluation that decides our conduct and our being reflects our values.